A Canine's Guide to the Good Life

Frankie, LuLu and Friends

With Donna Cavanagh

Copyright © 2013 by Frankie, LuLu and Friends
With Donna Cavanagh
All rights reserved. No part of this book may be used or reproduced in any manner whatsoever without written permission, except in the case of brief quotations embodied in critical articles or reviews.
Published 2013 by HumorOutcasts Press
Printed in the United States of America

ISBN 0-615-79217-0
EAN-13 978-061579217-0

To Grandpa Tozzi who on more than one occasion remarked: "These dogs--what a life! I want to come back as a dog in a family like this." Here's to making many more families like the ones we and our friends have.

Acknowledgements:

To the wonderful families who donated photos of their special pooches.

To the dogs we lost but still inspire us each day.

To Kelly Keebler for bringing order again into Frankie's life, and Hickory Veterinary Hospital who saved Frankie from parvo when she was a pup.

Bree O'Shell Lizana and Angel Pet Sitting (www.angelpetsitting.com) who take such good care of Frankie and LuLu when Mom and Dad have to be away!

To Beth Samarin, LuLu's and Frankie's Godmother! She thinks we're special.

To Nancy Berk and Deb Martin Webster for all their help!

How to Score an Owner

For many dogs, the prospect of finding the perfect owner is a daunting task. From the canine point of view, there are so many qualities to look for in a perspective human. It is only natural for all dogs, both puppies and adults, to be nervous about owner hunting. That is why we have put together a few rules to help you not only find the right human, but to mold that human into the owner you want him or her to be.

Rule # 1: If You Got Pedigree Flaunt It - Owners are divided into two groups: those who like surprises and those who do not. Pedigree owners do not like to go down the path of the unknown. So, if you are a pedigree pup and have the chops (we mean that figuratively) to prove it, do so. Bring out your papers which show your stellar blood lines or family history of wins at all the big shows. A good bloodline will help an owner justify the four-figure sticker shock that goes along with that bloodline. One caveat: If you are going to wave the pedigree papers under a human's nose, make sure that your bloodline was not sullied by your Uncle Scooter's dalliance with the Cockapoo down the street.

Rule # 2: Find the Owner Who Needs to Be Needed - If you are a mutt or in politically correct terminology, a "rescue", you will smell the need to be loved on a potential owner. It's best to play on that need. It would behoove you to look not only adorable, but a tad desperate too – nothing melts a potential rescue owner's heart like a tilted head and sad eyes. Add some kisses into that mix and you are in the car and headed to your new home. What mutts lack in pedigree, they make up for in the

Pedigree Posture - Bob Berk, a Chihuahua whose proud owner is Dr. Nancy Berk author of "College Bound and Gagged", recommends maintaining a regal posture, and a confident stare to capture the heart of a potential owner.

Research, Research, Research – Frankie and LuLu recommend background checks and income verification before committing to an owner.

"savior factor". New owners know they saved their mutts from an appointment with the vet version of Dr. Kevorkian. Rescue pups know they saved their owners from a life of complete boredom.

Sad Eyes and Tilt - Our cousins Phoebe and Zoey who live with Phyllis Tozzi, demonstrate the sad eyes/tilted head maneuver that can be used to score the perfect owner.

Rule # 3: Be Alert - Learn and practice the three P's when it comes to new owners: Preparation, Playful and Polite.

Preparation: Breeders, rescues and shelters always have busy times during the day when potential owners come to "browse". Figure out those busy times and plan your many naps around them. Those who snooze, lose. Prepare to be awake and on your best game. Peppy with a positive attitude goes a long way in capturing a human heart.

Playful: It's true that a sleeping dog looks adorable, but you need to show off your playful side to a potential owner, so he or she knows you will make a dandy companion. Potential owners will study not only you but every other dog that is around you. If the other dogs are showing off, so must you. Wag that tail, smile, rub your face with your paws (We don't know why, but humans love this), flip your ears around and shake your booty. Everything is fair in the quest to be adopted, so pull out all the stops.

Polite: Don't bite especially if you are not a pup. Puppies can get away with a little playful gnawing, but if you look like you enjoy it too much, you will make a human nervous. Also, even though we must do this at least once during the day, try not to poop, pass gas or piddle in front of potential owners. Hey, don't feel bad. Humans refrain from this stuff too when they are trying to reel in potential mates. While humans and beasts are aware that everyone has to perform these duties, we all must pretend that we don't until some type of commitment is reached. So, keep the bodily functions to a minimum until they say the magic words, "We'll take this one!" When you hear that phrase, let it rip.

How to Score Treats and Good Food

So, you got a home – what's next? Well, you have a lot of owner training to do. First on the list is training your owner to dole out the treats and food. Be patient in the treat process. Initially, owners listen to every word the "experts" say. Eventually, they will come around to your way of thinking.

Dog Food: At the beginning, they will only feed you the crap...uh, we mean the natural food with no filler that is made by communes in Canada and famous deceased actors who also make coffee and organic salad dressing. For treats you will get carrot and vegetable sticks recommended by the canine nutritionists who we in the canine community call "Food Fascists". When your owner relaxes a bit and gets tired of paying three times the amount for the designer treats over the regular treats, and they remember you are a dog who likes most anything, you will start to get the "good stuff" which can include anything from treats secretly stuffed with vitamins to rawhide bones to pig's ears to bacon treats to nylon bones that you just gnaw on forever but never truly eat.

People Food: Something else eventually occurs too. You might get your first taste of people food. Let us stress here that if you are unfortunate enough to have food allergies, there will be no people food, but if you are not an allergy sufferer, get ready. You might get a taste of steak or turkey or maybe tofu if you have vegetarian owners (Yeah, you won't like this). Some might scoff at vegetarian owners, but look at the bright side: you will never be looked upon as a new menu option if the economy tanks again.

What you will never get is a meat bone. Yes, the rumors you have heard about our ancestors pigging out (this is not a racist term meant to insult pigs) on meat bones is true. They got steak bones, rib bones...they got it all. But as it often happens in life, a few bad pooches ruin a good thing for the rest of us. Apparently, some canine klutzes did not understand the meaning of the term "gnaw". They not only chewed meat pieces off the bone, but they ate the bones too. This caused major gastric distress and some dogs even had to have surgery which inspired veterinarians everywhere to put the kibosh on real meat bones.

Pizza Delivery: Pay close attention to this: In a canine world, the pizza delivery person is a god. He or she brings heaven in a flat box. What can be so good in that box you say? Bread, cheese, sauce and if you live with a meat lover: sausage, a hybrid meat called pepperoni, meatballs, chicken...so many possibilities. And because pizza is a special food, there is a special way to approach eating it. The primary rule with pizza is that there are no rules. If you are an only dog, beg, roll over, pull out every page of your trick book - do whatever it takes to get that pizza. Once you get your first taste, you will know the humiliation was worth it. If you have dog siblings, do not be loyal or self-sacrificing. Where pizza is concerned, it is literally a dog-eat-dog world. You will understand this when you take your first taste of the magic pie.

A Canine's Guide to the Good Life

Pizza Nirvana – Our god is the guy who holds the pizza. Just pray he doesn't want the crust!
From left to right: Gryffin Berk (owners Nancy and Ron Berk); Maggie "Libby" and Tiger (owners Tom and Maria Woodward), and Jimmie Z (owners Roberta and Mark Czarnecki) demonstrate the right way to beg for pizza.

Coffee Table Snacks: Humans possess the strangest items. Probably, the most frustrating for canines is the furniture piece known as a coffee table. It is at our eye level, and on this table they put lots of wonderful food. But none of it...we repeat...none of it is for us. It is, in fact, the biggest tease we will face in our lives. You can slobber over the food on that table; you can stare down your owner hoping that he or she will allow you a taste, but it does not happen. For some reason that table is off limits for all canines. Your only hope at the coffee table food is if the owner exits the room and leaves the food unattended giving you a small window of opportunity to pounce.

Gregory, who lives with TV and film writer Mario Turchiarolo, contemplates his next move to retrieve the people food on the table.

Pouncing is a mistake. Why? Coffee table snacks tend to not be dog friendly. Often this food is spicy or not conducive to our digestive systems, and this can make us...how shall we put this gently...toot up a storm? Well, toot might not be a strong enough description. The food on the coffee table will fill you with so much gas that you could power a space shuttle mission. This might not sound bad except that the "fuel" you emit will send your family and yourself scurrying to the great outdoors for some much needed fresh air. Once outside, your humans might not be too anxious to let you back inside.

If you insist on going for the coffee table goodies, it might be best to learn the quick "side pass and grab". This is a complicated maneuver, and we don't recommend this for puppies. It takes maturity to pull this off. With the side pass and grab, you walk as close to the coffee table as possible and in one swift move, you turn your head quickly and grab a "human treat" in your mouth. As you get better at this, your owners might not even know you swiped food unless, of course, you steal something like a jalapeno popper. Yes, there is no hiding your reaction to anything with jalapeno. Your face will prove your guilt within seconds. So, the basic lesson is this: the coffee table might look inviting, but it's best to just leave it to the experienced canines or those whose mouths have no heat sensors.

Countertops: Everything on a countertop is fair game, and the countertop usually holds the best foods from cookies to those holiday rib roasts that for some reason wear little booties. Don't ask us why dead meat needs footwear. It's a human thing. For some reason humans like their meat to look cute before they slice through it, chew it and digest it. Anyway, your owners might not think that you have rights to the countertop, but they are wrong. We know better. The best way to access the food on the counter is to hoist yourself up on your hind legs and grab onto the countertop with your front paws. This will allow you a quick look to see if there is anything up there that you find appetizing.

Let's assume there is a roast beef sitting on the counter cooling and waiting to be sliced. Yes, we know the aroma will drive you crazy, but caution is needed here. Check to see where your humans are in the house or even if they are home. If they left the roast alone with you, they deserve no pity; that roast is yours. If they are home, you have to weigh the roast against potential punishment. Even though you were left alone with a warm, succulent roast and you are a dog, an owner might think you should have showed some restraint before poaching that meat. What humans do not get, and we can't stress this enough, is that we are not humans; we are dogs. Cooked meat left within our snout's reach will be eaten without an ounce of guilt. We will even eat raw meat. As carnivores, we are happy to eat it anyway it is presented. This is how we are made.

If you are a considerate pooch, you can take a chomp out of the meat and leave a portion for your family, but what's the point of that? Your family will not eat your leftovers. They have a thing about dog saliva touching their food, so if you are going to steal the meat, steal the entire thing. You are still going to get in trouble so you might as well go for the whole enchilada—that's a figure of speech. Don't eat enchiladas.

Countertop Food to Avoid: Do not eat chocolate cake, brownies, chocolate candy, ant traps that smell like peanut butter, grapes, raisins and onions. These are not dog-friendly foods and if you eat them, you might wind up at the vet again feeling embarrassed and sick.

Co-author Frankie - knows there is good stuff on the countertop but the countertop is technically off limits.

Fast Food: If you have really indulgent owners, you might find yourself placing an order in the drive-thru window at your local fast food restaurant. If you are lucky enough to live where they have drive-in restaurants like Sonic, you get the royal treatment and someone from the restaurant brings your burgers to your car. While this food is a special treat, we must warn you that the drive-thrus and drive-ins are not for the inexperienced pooch. We will teach you the ropes for these restaurants in a later chapter on Road Trip Etiquette.

The Tricks-For-Treat Dance: The Tricks-For-Treat Dance has nothing to do with Halloween, the holiday that sends many a dog to the brink of insanity with all the doorbell rings and scary people coming to the house in masks--some brandishing weapons. We don't get Halloween. On every other day of the year, if strangers come to the door wearing masks and brandishing weapons, our owners would want us to tear their arms off. On Halloween, we are supposed to like them and give them food. It's all very confusing. Sorry, we have issues with Halloween; let's move on.

For dogs, Tricks-for-Treats is our normal everyday life. We want a snack, we do a trick. Our owners get to pretend that they are in control, but they aren't. We know how to perform to maximize their treat output. In case you are a young pup not yet familiar with the Tricks-for-Treat tradition, allow us to fill you in.

When looking to score treats, always remember that manners are important. For some reason, owners want their canines to be polite, gentle and grateful for the treats. It's a small price to pay to get a tasty doggie delight. Yes, it's embarrassing, but if you perform the tricks the right way, you get to put the treat supply in your control. For example, your owner will wave a treat in front of your nose and say "Sit" in a definitive tone. You will sit, and you will get a treat. Now, stay seated and do the "tilt your head" trick that got you adopted in the first place. That tilt never gets old, and if you do opt to tilt, treat number two will be in your stomach before you know it. Then, finish off your owner's resistance by extending your paw without being asked. You have just earned a third treat. Repeat until you are full. Use your imagination and come up with tricks they have not taught you: dance, twirl, hop or roll over. Your owner will be so enthralled with your tricks, they will shower you in treats. They might even let you select the treats you want. Don't be surprised if some dogs consider this behavior "selling out", but those dogs don't have a cupboard filled with a variety of rawhides or bacon strips waiting to be devoured.

Bones – Remy, a Jack Russell Terrier who lives with the O'Connor family in Upstate NY, shows off his tricks-for-treats reward.

What to Do if You Don't Like the Food your Human serves:
When presented with a bowl of food you do not like, you need to take action so your owner understands that the food is unacceptable. There are subtle ways to get this message across.

Dig your nose deep into your bowl and scoop the food with your snout and push it onto the floor. If you do this two or three times, your owner will understand that you are not pleased. For those dogs who get wet or canned food, scooping out your food can be trickier and messier, but your owners will get your dissatisfaction quickly and switch foods as no one, not even canines, like to step in wet dog food tossed around a room.

If your owner just thinks you are a messy eater after dumping some of the food onto the floor, you must demonstrate your displeasure in other ways. Take a mouthful of food and dump it in your water bowl. This tends to gross out your owners as the food gets soft and expands with moisture, and for some reason it also smells more. You know, it's funny. We dogs upchuck a lot, but owners gag, dry heave or projectile vomit easily when they are faced with not-so-pleasant-looking and not-so-pleasant smelling doggie stuff. A few days of cleaning up discarded wet food will have your owners gagging all day long and ready to make a change. Sorry, but this was an important observation about humans we thought we should share. Now, back to the food. If the tossing of the food onto the floor or into the water bowl does not work, you might have to place little piles of food on the furniture or on the floors in other rooms where your food bowl is not in view. Carrying food around and not eating it will remind your owners that you are not enjoying the cuisine they provide. If all else fails, scarf down the food really fast so that it comes back up equally as fast in big chunks and deposit the not-quite-digested food on their favorite Oriental area rug or in the middle of their bed. Nothing gets attention faster than chunky dog vomit.

Rocky (LuLu's brother), who lives with the Tozzi family, demonstrates the food to water bowl transfer and really gets into it.

What have we learned in this chapter? On the surface, it might seem that dogs have no say in what food and treats they get from owners, but trust us, with a little ingenuity, we can eat the food we want when we want.

Your House Your Way

Dog owners think their canines adjust to their human home, but in truth, dogs make a house THEIR home. This does not occur overnight, and this is a good thing because you want this transition to be gradual, so gradual that your owners never realize that their house has gone to the dogs.

Some ways to bring your personal touch to your human's home:

Blankets: Make your owners get lots of blankets. Before humans become dog owners, they see blankets as bed accessories or decorative accents for a couch or chair. After dog ownership, blankets can be found on every piece of furniture in the house. Why? Well, humans think it's because we shed. However, we know that if we make our hair and fur fall off, humans will get blankets to protect their furniture, and we get to be comfy and cozy all day long.

Lucy, a rescued Pit Bull who lives with Ginny Simon of Project Marketing, Inc., likes her blankets pink and soft.

But what type of blanket is good for a dog? Frankly, the choice is yours. "How do we buy what we like?" some of you might ask. Simple. Each time the humans bring home a blanket that displeases your sense of style, chew it up. The same goes for those stupid decorative pillows people insist on owning. Keep doing this until your human finds a blanket or pillow that is easy on your eyes. Do the same to the furniture. A word of caution here: Humans go berserk if there is too much property damage, so wisely pick and choose what furniture to destroy.

Rocky, a Cavalier King Charles Spaniel owned by Mary Lou Quinlan, New York Times bestselling author of *The God Box* and her husband Joe, creates his own style with his favorite fabric choice for his NYC home.

Window Spit: Window spit is one of the most personal décor additions you can provide as a canine. Window spit is both beautiful and functional – at least to dogs. It's a dog's calling card to strangers to let them know a canine is on the premises, and the more spit you leave on the window, the better your street "cred" in the neighborhood becomes. At first, your owners will wipe the spit off the window on a daily basis. Then, it becomes a weekly ritual. After your owner goes through two to three bottles of Windex and enough paper towels to make even the least tree-hugging person feel environmentally guilty, he or she will re-evaluate the spit and see it not as a physical reminder of dog germs but as a practical art medium that serves as a privacy barrier against nosy neighbors. A good dog can layer his spit work so it is three to four inches thick on any window. It is an added feather in your cap if you can make your spit turn crusty...the crustier the better. When your spit becomes as tough to remove as permanent marker, your perfect piece of pet art is complete. Once your owners recognize your artistic flair, they will view your work as wispy clouds of canine love and not curse in disgust each time the sun hits your windows and highlights the spit's existence. And one last advantage to the spit: The cloudy windows give birds on the outside of the house the heads up that they are flying into a solid surface thus allowing them a few extra seconds to alter their flight path before they go splat.

Window Views: While we are on the topic of windows, dogs love windows—the bigger the better. If you are lucky enough to have a French door or sliding glass door as your window to the world, you're living the good life. A full-glass door not only provides you a great view of the critters and nature outside, but a strong warm sunbeam for you to enjoy while resting on the inside. If your house does not have a full glass door, get your owner to place a sofa or chair in front of the window to increase your view and sunbeam exposure. A good owner will also recognize the value of a canine window perch. A window perch can show anyone who is up to no good in the neighborhood that you guard your home and are prepared to take action if they get too close to your perimeter. You can also use your window seat to check out the other dogs on the block when they take their owners for a walk. It's good to get to know the other dogs and share doggie gossip. Also, from your prime viewing location, you can see the "cool" kids walk to and from the school bus and you can bark "hello". Even the coolest kids wave back.

Toby, whose owner is TV producer and novelist Bruce Ferber, author of *Elevating Overman*, enjoys the ocean views while Ferber sweats out his second novel nearby.

Windows give you a ringside view of the mailman, UPS guy, and other delivery people as they approach, and you can greet them with an eager and loud voice. Don't be insulted if these fine folks don't appear appreciative of your presence and/or loud voice. It's another human thing. However, your owners will appreciate your enthusiastic greetings at the window because your barks will chase away salesmen, politicians and religious groups looking for donations or an opportunity to save your owners' souls.

Nancy Vallow, Goldendoodle of TV producer Kara Vallow, not only greets the mailman with a crisp bark but dresses up to show she understands his tough job.

We should also point out the one negative of a booming greeting in the window. You might frighten away Girl Scouts during their cookie campaign. So, if you see little female humans dressed in green or brown, keep down the noise--the cookies are worth it.

Maggie, the Wheaten Terrier, who rules the roost in the Craig Wilson/Jack Cahill household in Washington D.C., shows us her tough stance by the doorway that keeps the mailman, UPS guy and the FedEx delivery man on their toes.

Beds: Beds can be a dog's best friend and an owner's worst nightmare. Some owners love to have their dogs on their beds; others find it disgusting. Don't judge too harshly the owners who refuse to share their beds with their pets.

They could have allergies or maybe dog hair makes them itchy or maybe they feel as if a dog ruins the potential for romance with other humans. Humans are funny creatures. They don't understand that we don't care what they do with other humans. We just want the bed.

There is a certain amount of bed etiquette that you, as a dog, should follow:

*Don't steal the covers
*Don't slobber on the pillows
*If there is any activity between humans going on, don't stare; it breaks their concentration and then they get cranky.
*Don't piddle or poop. It's just rude.

Rosie, the little Chihuahua with a big bark, who lives with the Buongervino family in Pennsylvania, makes it known that the king-size bed in her home belongs to her first and the people second.

Your Own Bed: Some dogs do not like to share a bed with humans and prefer their own space. Some settle in a guest room while other dogs have their own beds. Dog beds come in a variety of shapes and sizes. Small dog owners tend to get fancier beds for their little canines. The cost of a bed grows as a dog grows, so if you are a 150-pound brute, don't expect a doggie canopy bed with real brass accents; expect an oversized pillow for the floor. A dog bed does not have to be fancy; it just has to tell the world that this is your space and your space only.

"It's my bed, and I sit wherever I want," says Toby Ferber.

Crates: Some dogs hate their crates while others never outgrow them. Some view their crates as their own special house within the human house that brings with it an added sense of security, and there are many of us who need that extra sense of security. There is no reason to be ashamed if you still use your crate into your adult years, and if the other dogs in the neighborhood poke fun at you, they are not worth your time. A crate should not diminish your standing in the canine community.

Co-Author Frankie loves her crate especially when there is a nice blanket at the bottom.

Toys, Tennis Balls and Games

If you are a puppy, you will think everything from shoes to socks to toilet paper are toys. But the sad truth is NONE of these are toys, and if you steal them from your owner, you will get into trouble, and what is worse, if you eat them--especially the socks--you might have to make another unscheduled trip to the vet. Yes, that vet is always ready for you! So what does a dog do for entertainment?

Kaley, whose mom is former D.A. and novelist Robin Lamont author of *Wright for America* and a new suspense series about an animal welfare investigator, shows that it's sometimes tough to choose between a good toy and a good back rub.

Stuffed Toys: A good toy for us used to be a stuffed object that was shaped like a cat, mailman or bone. In truth, the shape didn't matter. What was cool about them was that we could tear them to shreds. It was wonderful. We chewed until fluff flew out. The pleasure from this toy reached its height when we found the squeaker in the center and pulled it out with our teeth. It was pure fun.

A Canine's Guide to the Good Life

Marcel, the prized pooch of writer and producer Laurie Gelman, demonstrates the pride a dog feels when locating the squeaker at the center of a toy.

But in the last few years, the annoying dog experts said that toy stuffing is bad for us. This negative review of our beloved toys was reinforced when a few of our not-so-intelligent canines ate the fun squeaker at the center, which put a crimp in their digestive systems and forced more vet visits. So now the experts have introduced flat toys with no stuffing and no squeakers. From a dog's point of view, these are not toys; they are just socks with faces. The funny thing about these new toys is we are not supposed to play with socks; so, what is the point of the flat toy? While we are protesting toys, be aware that dog toy manufacturers have come up with a new idea: interactive toys that are designed to teach us life skills. Why do we need life skills? Are we going to school or getting a job? No, unless you are a service dog or a K-9 cop, you have no job outside the house with the exception of catching and killing a few critters in the yard.

Owners will try and convince you that all activities are play, but you have to be careful not to fall into their trap. Here are some games you can initiate with your owner that might not make *them* laugh, but they will provide you with hours of merriment.

Faking Fetch: Every dog gets a tennis ball or Frisbee at some point in his or her life. Apparently, everyone from Santa to the Easter Bunny to the Birthday Elf (yes, our mom says there is one), brings these objects. Let's face it; they are the perfect toys, and if used correctly, they provide entertainment for both dogs and humans. We can chew on them or chase them or play fetch with them. Some dogs love to play fetch for hours. Others do not want to play fetch at all. If you don't like to retrieve the tennis ball or Frisbee, you can still enjoy this game by watching your human retrieve it over and over again.

Muffie – a German Shepherd mix who lived with the Cavanaghs before Frankie and LuLu, was an expert at fetching tennis balls. Frankie and LuLu--not so much.

This is what you do: take a tennis ball and drop it in front of your owner's feet. Watch your human throw the ball but do not make a move toward the ball. Just sit there and look disinterested and aloof. Your owner will eventually give in and retrieve the ball for you. You will probably get your owner to do this about six or seven times before he or she gets the message you are not chasing that ball. The funny thing about owners is that they will continue to try and teach you the game of fetch. You might never fetch a ball, but your owner will become very obedient and fetch lots of stuff besides tennis balls for you. Once your owner is obedient, you can call the shots on everything from when to eat, sleep and poop or whatever makes your fur fly.

Hiding the TV Remote: Humans, especially men, think they own the TV remote. If you want any shot at watching your TV shows, you need to learn to hide the remote for ONE TV – the biggest TV in the house. This is important. If you hide all the remotes, the humans will know, you are to blame, but if you hide only ONE remote, they will think they put it down somewhere and forgot. Eventually, they will just give up and go to another room to watch their shows rather than waste time trying to locate the lost remote. This is perfect. Once they are comfortable, you get the sofa, the blankets and the big screen all to yourself.

Ghost in the House Game: To start: Growl at the air. This freaks humans out. Why? If you growl at the air for no reason, your owners will think you are seeing ghosts. Yep, that is the conclusion they will jump to; trust us. Apparently, dogs, cats and kids have the inside track on the paranormal and "experts" say a dog barking at nothing is seeing spirits. This game can keep your owners preoccupied for months if you master it. This is how the game is played. 1) Pick your head up as if someone walks into the room; 2) Start to emit a low grumble that says, "I am confused and a little scared."

Then, do your best timid look. You can tremble a bit or place your tail between your legs. 3) Turn that low grumble into a fierce growl (the same growl you use on the mailman). 4) Then yelp and run under a bed and refuse to come out. Your humans will be so freaking scared! It's a riot. The best part is that not only will you spook your owners into near insanity, but they will feel badly that the spirits are harassing you and give you steak. Yes, it's a mean con, but we are talking steak, so all is fair when meat is involved.

Gryffin Berk, pulls off his best "Oooh, I see a ghost!" face for his parents Ron and Nancy Berk.

Make Them Teach You Tricks: Every puppy and dog goes through some training especially for treats. However, training can turn into entertainment for you and give you bragging rights at the dog park too. Here is how it works: When your owner tells you to sit, stay or give your paw for a treat, do it. Once they think you have mastered these basic tricks, they will move on to more complicated commands like "twirl" and "roll over". And this is where the fun begins.

Pretend not to get these commands at first or that you forgot them. Sit there and look confused. Tilt your head to emphasize your confusion. Then watch and be ready to laugh for it is at this point that owners will demonstrate how the trick is done. They will twirl, dance, roll over, play dead, sing in a barky tone--whatever the trick they want you to do, they will do first. You will pee on the floor because you will laugh so hard. (Okay, try not to pee on the floor because that kills the fuzzy buzz the owner feels during training sessions). And like Fetch, watching your humans do tricks could provide months of entertainment. After a while, the humans will stop performing and the games will end, but it was fun while it lasted.

Young Nancy Vallow shows off her sitting, posing and staying skills.

How to Be Fashion Forward

As your dog mentors, we feel it is our duty to keep you up to date on canine fashion trends. Fashion for dogs is relatively new for the dog world. When our ancestors lived in the wild, they had no fashion. As we learned to co-exist and love humans, they seemed to want us to love their clothes as much as they do. Go with it! At first, it was just Poodle owners who possessed the desire to get their dogs a cute haircut, sparkly collars and a designer dress. But other breed owners followed suit. Now, all dogs, big or small, show off trendy doggie wear with dresses, coats, sweaters, hats, scarves, themed collars and bling. Fashion for canines is serious business and all dogs, be they mutts or pedigrees, sport the latest fads in pet apparel. While colors and fabrics change from year to year, there are staples that every dog should have in their wardrobe that can take them from daytime to an evening out.

Bandanas: Bandanas say, "I am the dog. I am self-assured, laid back and really, really cool." When owners have more than one dog, they tend to make them wear matching bandanas. Human kids hate matching clothes, but dog kids don't seem to mind. We like that look actually. Bandanas can be made for holidays, birthdays and special events. Owners can get bandanas to show off their favorite school or sports team, and as far as clothing goes, they are the least expensive. Lots of plusses for bandanas, so if your owner puts one on you, strut your stuff.

Phoebe models the patriotic bandana look that all dogs can rock.

Bows: Groomers love bows – unfortunately, they even like them on boy dogs, and some male dogs are not thrilled with the bows especially when they are trying to sniff out which female dog is "ready" for companionship, Boy dogs don't want to look pretty. They want to look studly. Bows used to be reserved for the toy dog breeds, but now even St. Bernard dogs come back from the groomer with the froufrou bows. Their owners think they look cute, take pictures and post them on Facebook. But if you are a big dog and you have bows and your picture is on Facebook, the other dogs are going to see it and your reputation is shot. The only thing you can do is shake the bows off your head or pick a fight with another dog who will bite them off your ears. It's worth the blood.

Tutu Skirts and Hats: Once again, on a toy dog, a frilly tutu looks cute--odd but cute. Try to put that on a big dog and it just becomes animal abuse. Hats can be tolerated for certain occasions. Every dog likes to wear a tiara once in a while. It's good for our confidence. We will also tolerate headwear for the holidays and special occasions, but big dogs do not want sweaters or coats. Much like our human female, perimenopausal owners, too many layers make us uncomfortable, hot and grouchy. At this time, we would like to ask the humans a question? Why are you buying us designer duds? We don't know a Burberry coat from a Walmart brand. What the hell is wrong with you people?

Gryffin and Bob Berk prove that accessories don't make the dogs; dogs make the accessories!

Dog Strollers: We were not sure what category to put doggie strollers in, so we are just listing it in its own category. We canines don't get doggie strollers. Why? Well, the obvious answer is that we are dogs. Have some dignity and walk even if your human owners do not think you can walk. A dog in a stroller is humiliating. If you insist on or are forced to ride in a stroller, make your owner get that netting thing that keeps bugs away. At least if you have this bit of camouflage, and you pass other dogs, they can't see that it is you in the stroller. Even if they do get a quick peek, they will just think they saw a really ugly human baby. Hey, we get that you humans want to spoil us and we are okay with that, but please try not to lose your grip on reality in this relationship. Save the strollers for your own offspring.

Jimmie Z models holiday headgear and a coordinating collar and proves that fashion is essential in ringing in the holiday spirit.

Road Trip Etiquette

We all yearn to hear the car keys jingle and our owners say, "Wanna go for a ride?" The car for a dog is the ultimate vacation. Humans can just take us around the block but if the window is open and our snouts are hanging out, we are happy indeed. Believe it or not, to make the car ride, either long or short, a positive experience for both humans and canines, there are some rules we must follow:

Wear a Seat Belt: Yes, doggies have seat belts and it's a good idea to suggest these to your owner. When you get a seat belt, do not try to wriggle out of it and put yourself in a choke hold. This requires owners to pull off to the side of the road and help you breathe again. Be a cooperative passenger, and the car rides will be more frequent.

Duke, who serves as head of security for Stocomo Ranch in Stone County, Missouri rides shotgun and enjoys his front seat view.

Sharing: If you have to share the backseat with another dog or human kids, be generous. You can't spread out and take up the entire seat. Pay attention to the human ones in the seat next to you especially the babies. Smile at them or kiss them but do not lick their stuff. We don't know why kisses are good but licking their stuff is bad to humans, but it is.

Co-Authors LuLu and "baby Frankie" snuggle on a trip to Grandma's.

Who is the Driver? Always remember you are a passenger in the car. You are never to drive. Your paws do not reach the right pedals, and you don't have thumbs to hold onto the wheel correctly. You can help out your owner though if you notice he or she displays poor driving skills. Learn to bark at yellow lights to tell him or her to slow down. Growl if they text or talk on their cell phone, and if they smoke, pretend you can't breathe so they put the cigarette out.

Nausea: If you are a dog who gets queasy in a car, ask for a window seat at all times, and if you must purge do it on the floor. If you want your owners to learn that you do not like the car, we suggest that you purge on the front console that is right next to the driver or passenger. They will get your point and you will gain sympathy as long as you do not try and re-eat what you lost. Humans love us, but they do not get our need to re-ingest what our body has released. Go figure!

Windows: Feel free to stick your snout out the window. We know you want to get the wind in your ears, but be careful of this. A bad turn by your human or flying objects thrown out the window by someone else on the road can lead to injury. Be smart with your head; it's the only one you have.

While your head is out the window, feel free to say hello to other people in other cars. A smiling dog enjoying a car ride makes humans smile. Again, don't throw up in another car's direction. You lose the cute factor.

Drive Thru: At toll booths and fast food or bank drive thrus, be quiet and polite – especially at the banks where they give you treats for being good pooches. When your owner takes you to a fast food place, do not bark your orders into the speaker. Let your owner speak for you. Don't feel badly, the people on the other end of the speaker in the restaurant can barely make out what human customers say into those speakers, so Dogspeak is impossible for them to understand. When your food arrives, don't jump on it. Be patient especially if you are not an only dog. The more calm everyone is in the car, the more your owner will take you for rides to the food joints. If there are food fights or growls or general misbehaving, you will stay home when your humans go in the car. If you go to someplace like Sonic Drive-in where food is brought to you, do not scare the servers. Let them deliver your food without you trying to steal the fries out of their hands or barking at them to move faster. Servers do not like barking dogs. Do not be a bully and wait for your food to be handed to you.

Destination Rides: Sometimes dogs go in the car for a purpose. You have to go to the groomer, the pet store or the vet. Yes, the vet. This should not ruin your ride or send you into a panic. We all need the vet a few times per year, and if you are really good and don't whine in the car especially when you recognize the route to the vet, your owner will most likely give you a treat and maybe that treat is a ride through the fast food drive-thru.

Vet Visits: Let's take an opportunity to talk about the vet. The vet is your friend. The routine at the vet is very simple: They weigh you, listen to your lungs, look at your ears and teeth and then sometimes you get shots. The shots don't really hurt, but they can make you sleepy which turns into a vacation day for your owner. Be nice to the vet as they decide when you live and when you go to Hound Heaven. And guess what, vets love us almost as much as our owners love us, so why mess with that?

The Great Outdoors

Most dogs love the outdoor life. We love to run around our yards or walk in the park no matter what weather Mother Nature has delivered. While we see the great outdoors as a place of ultimate freedom, please note that there are definite rules that all dogs must abide by to earn their playtime out in the open.

Thunder Bear, a member of the Bob Sleasman/Rich Ostreicher household, smiles as the wind hits his face while on the open road.

Be Civil to Other Dogs: This is a difficult thing to do. We tend to want to show everyone that we are the "best" dog in the world. We know this is true because our owners tell us so, but we don't understand how the rest of the world is unaware of this fact. Another point: Each dog is different. Not all of us want to be social with a million dogs, so go at your own pace. Remember our mantra: A happy dog is a calm dog. When you meet a dog and you sense that dog wants to get to know you, you can begin the sniffing process. But be polite: No behind sniffing until a formal introduction has been made. This is especially true in a dog park. Sometimes dogs forget their manners and start a hind-quarters-sniffing Congo line. While it might seem natural for us, it makes our humans cringe a bit. So keep it classy.

Do Not Fantasize about Other Owners: This is a common mistake many canines make when they meet other dogs in public venues. They see how other humans are and they wonder what it would be like to be their pets. They hear other dogs talking about their special dog foods, homemade treats and lavish days at the dog spa or the new teacher at doggy day care and they think, "Wow, that dog has a great life!" Before you go down that fantasy road, look around and see what you have. Remember, the fire hydrant on the other side of the street is always shinier until you get up close, and then you realize it's pretty much the same as the one on your side.

Daisy Blizzard maintains a protective mode for her owner, comedian Dena Blizzard (OneFunnyMother.com), while Coco scouts for a new owner who might fit his tastes better.

Do not Scare Away Birds: A lot of yards have bird feeders. This is where our feathered friends find refreshment and some rest. Birds are our friends except for hawks who like to dive bomb us and scare the crap out of us. Let birds be a part of your yard. They sing pretty songs and add a sense of serenity to our backyard existence.

Wild Critters Are a No No: Wild critters should be avoided and/or ignored if possible. They are dangerous and spell trouble for you and your family.

Skunks – If you get too close to a skunk, they will spritz you with foul-smelling stuff and you will not see your family up close and personal for days. No bath gets the stench of skunk out completely. You may think you can take on a skunk, but don't chance it.

Groundhogs, Woodchucks, Opossums, Raccoons – same warning as the skunks. They might not smell but they have claws that will make you wish you just got sprayed by a skunk. Stay clear at all costs.

Bunnies – Sure they look harmless and fluffy, but they are evil--pure evil. They want to eat your owner's vegetable garden and will stop at nothing to get at that food supply. Everyone sees a bunny and thinks, "How cute", but when it's you and the bunny face-to-face, the bunny will show you its devilish side. Why do you think magicians like them so much? They con everyone from innocent children to felons into thinking they are cuddly and loving.

Snakes, Mice, Rats and Assorted Little Rodents – Do not bring them home as trophies to your humans. Humans will not recognize or applaud your efforts. They will just emit loud screams and slam the door in your face.

Snow Play: Dogs love the snow, and our humans love that we love the snow. For some reason, a dog with his snout covered in the white stuff sends our owners over the edge and in search of cameras. They take pictures of us digging in the snow, eating the snow, peeing in the snow, and barking at snowmen standing in the snow – you name it if there is snow involved, there is a photograph.

Oso, the newest member of the Tozzi family enjoys a romp in the snow, a first-time experience for the rescue puppy.

Truth be told, this will not upset you. For those who have not had the opportunity to play in snow yet, you have a treat in store for you. Snow is invigorating; it gets your heart racing and your legs dancing, It's also the only time that if you knock your humans down, they don't seem to care. They laugh at it. We haven't quite figured out why they laugh at falling in the snow, but they don't laugh when we knock them down the steps, Humans are strange.

Co-author LuLu Cavanagh leaps for joy when it snows.

Walks: Taking your owner for a walk is a time-honored tradition between human and canine. You will have to attach them to a leash. Sure they will think they are in charge on the walk, but let them have that fantasy. Why should you want a walk? Well, if you are a city dog, a good walk gives you the opportunity to stretch your legs and see the world outside your apartment. If you are a suburban or country dog, a walk gives you a chance to check out your "hood" and chat with the other dogs who bark at you from their yards.

Humans do not realize that conversation between dogs is essential to maintaining the fabric of a neighborhood. One walk around the block tells a dog who is friendly, who has cats and who is wanted by the cops. Never underestimate a good walk and always be willing to share your knowledge with your fellow canines.

Crazy Things Our Owners Do

Owners love to spoil us, and we like to be spoiled. Sometimes, an owner can go overboard but unless their actions are totally humiliating, go with it. Always, remember, that they mean well. Here are some of the silliest actions humans will perform because they think they make our lives better:

They Leave on Music or the TV When They Go Out: Our humans feel badly when we are alone in the house. They leave on anything that makes noise so that we think we are not alone. We usually can tell the difference between a TV, radio and real live voices, but it's a sweet gesture, so we pretend to like it.

Years ago, the dogs who were here before us would say that their owners left messages for them on something called an answering machine. They would call the house from a far off place and talk to us through that machine. Now, we have voicemail, and the machine is gone. This is sad, but there are still some human parents who call and leave messages anyway. We think it's because they think we know the code to access their voicemail. If you have one of these humans, Love them; they are special.

They Install Alarm Systems That Do Not Comfort Us: Computer activated alarm systems that turn on lights and appliances when no one is home are NOT fun for us. This remote control capability literally scares the poop out of us.

Okay, I guess this "smart technology" might be payback for the "Ghost in the House" game we play on them, but humans should really know better and not delight in our fear.

They Offer Loud Noise Comfort: Who amongst us is not afraid of thunder, fireworks or other loud noises? Some of us have a great deal of fear when loud noises sound while others worry less. Owners have come up with their own remedies to keep us calm when loud sounds invade our space.

Thunder, a dog with a perfect name for this chapter, sports both headphones and a toy to keep him company.

Coats that mimic an owner hugging us – We have all seen these garments and we must say that they do make many dogs feel better. However, after a while, they can get annoying to put on. Many dogs would rather be naked and face their fears than be wrapped up for hours at a time waiting for a storm to pass through. However, we do think the hugging coat makes owners feel better about storms, so if you can tolerate the hugging coat, wear it for them.

Maybe one day, they will make a human one to hug them as well.

Headphones - Some owners think if they put headphones on us, we will not hear the loud boom booms from outside. We are dogs with hearing that can pick up a rattle of a treat box three streets over; the headphones are not going to work, but they make us look really cute.

Singing songs through loud noises - Yes, some humans will sing to us when they think we are afraid. This is not comforting unless they can carry a tune. If you have humans whose "dulcet" tones emit such a high frequency that cats in the next county complain, you will not appreciate their singing nor will you find comfort. The only way to avoid "human help" during loud noise episodes is to go under--under a table, under a bed, under anything. Remember, the operative word in Thunder is *Under*. Find a safe place and your human will relax too.

They Read Our Minds and Talk for Us: For some reasons, humans believe if dogs could talk, our voices would be either very high pitched if we are female and very low pitched if we are male, and all our "L's" and "R's" sound like "W's". Don't get mad at these stereotypes. Blame it on Scooby Doo. Scooby was the only example of Dogspeak humans had for a long time, so they accepted his speech as fact. Is it bad if our human speaks for us? No, usually they are on target with what we are thinking, and we come off cute in the voiceover which can lead to treats. So, let them have fun.

They Will Try and Pretend You Are Human and Believe You Can Adapt to Their Lives: This is silly since we expect humans to adapt to our lives. For example, we canines are creatures of habit. We get up at the same time each morning and want to go out in the yard or go for a walk. Many owners think that when Saturday rolls around, we should know that it is the weekend and we should want to sleep in. This is not going to work. We don't sleep in. The sooner you get your owner to understand that we don't care what day of the week it is, the better life will be for everyone.

They Make You Picture Perfect: Okay, raise your paws if you have ever had to pose for a professional or staged photo with or without your family. Yes, there are a lot of paws up I bet. Holiday photos, birthday photos, Halloween photos, graduation photos--pet photos are such a big thing that there are photographers who actually make a great living making us pose for the camera. How did this occur? We blame it on the guy who made the "Dogs Playing Poker" picture so famous. I guess the human world thought that if dogs can play cards, we can wear hats and look cheery for photos.

Zoe Mayhem, a three-legged wonder, is the picture of perfection and lives with British radio DJ Neal Mayhem who is founder of MinutesofMayhem.com and author of *The Mourning DJ*.

How to be a Great Dog

In this book, we have tried to show you how to achieve the good life. Now, it's time for us to share with you what you can do to help your owners achieve the good life.

Love Your Owner: We are one of the only creatures on Earth that give unconditional love. This is why humans want us. They know that no matter what they throw our way, we want to love them back, so when they come home after a long day of work, slobber them with kisses and affection. It sets the tone for the rest of the day.

Stay in Your Yard: We know that the outside world looks inviting and adventurous, but leaving your owner's home can only bring trouble. Do not dig under fences to escape or decide to tour the neighborhood on your own.

Respect Your Owner's Life: In recent years, we have seen a lot more owners work from home. Work is the thing they do to make money to feed us and buy us toys and treats. If you have an owner who is working from home, do not interrupt their day by barking when they are on the phone or demanding hugs when they are trying to work at the computer. Do not paw the keyboard and send email that should not be sent or delete email that should not be deleted.

Honey, who lives with Mystery Lovers Bookshop owner Laurie Miller Stephens and acts as her personal assistant, knows that paws on the keyboard can lead to trouble.

Stay Out of the Trash: That big barrel of trash in the kitchen looks inviting, but this is sort of a trap that you should not fall into. Remember, if you are alone in the house and the trash goes over, you are the main suspect or at least the main canine of interest. If you have fellow doggie siblings, you might be able to shift blame, but we dogs are very bad liars and our faces reveal our guilt without much prompting. So, if you don't want to hear the words "Bad dog!" don't be one.

Human Love: Humans want to love dogs, and we want to love humans. It's the perfect relationship, and it comes with

Graham who lives with Chuck Sambuchino, author of Red Dog/Blue Dog: When Pooches Get Political (reddog-bluedog.com), is an expert at making his owner laugh out loud.

rewards. We get a good home, and our owners get better checkups at their human vets. When we love them, they laugh more, their blood pressure goes down and life is good. So, give your owners a few hugs a day and let them know they can count on you.

Just Be You: Each human has his or her unique personality that makes us love them...not always understand them...but love them. This is why we picked them to be our owners. So, be yourself and accept your human's strengths and weaknesses and you too can have the good life and rule the roost. And if you still have questions about training your humans, we have one suggestion left:

ASK A CAT! THEY KNOW HOW TO GET THE JOB DONE!

Corporal Freckles who lives with Deb Martin-Webster, author of *Love, Montana,* rules her house; she can teach you to rule yours too.

We know that the dogs in this book live a wonderful life and we also know that many are out there searching for that life, so a portion of our royalties are going to pet charities to help dogs everywhere find their perfect home.